Creating —

FLOWER DISPLAYS

Creating
FLOWER DISPLAYS

Easy ideas for fresh
and lasting arrangements

JENNY RAWORTH

PHOTOGRAPHY BY JOHN HESELTINE

NEW HOLLAND

First published in 2002 by

New Holland Publishers (UK) Ltd

London · Cape Town · Sydney · Auckland

Garfield House

86-88 Edgware Road

London W2 2EA

United Kingdom

www.newhollandpublishers.com

80 McKenzie Street

Cape Town 8001

South Africa

Level 1, Unit 4, 14 Aquatic Drive

Frenchs Forest, NSW 2086

Australia

218 Lake Road

Northcote, Auckland

New Zealand

10 9 8 7 6 5 4 3 2 1

ISBN 1-84330-008-7 (HB)

A BERRY BOOK

Conceived, edited and designed by Susan Berry

47 Crewys Road

London NW2 2AU

Senior editor: Clare Hubbard

Production: Hazel Kirkman

Editorial direction: Rosemary Wilkinson

Designer: Anne Wilson

Reproduction by PICA Digital PTE Ltd, Singapore

Printed and bound in Malaysia by Times Offset (M) Sdn. Bhd.

CONTENTS

introduction

There is no more successful way to turn a house into a home than by using floral decoration of one sort or another. But instead of the elaborate arrangements of yesteryear, people now want beautiful, simple arrangements that look natural, even if they are not. In the past, flowers formed the centrepiece of any decoration but increasingly attention has turned to form and texture, so that foliage in all its forms has become a popular ingredient in floral decoration. Slender grasses, either fresh or dried, make simple yet elegant arrangements for modern interiors.

In addition to the wealth of hedgerow material at our disposal – from rosehips to pyracantha berries, from vines to crab apples – there is an increasingly sophisticated range of artificial foliage, flowers and fruit, from silk tulips to plastic cherries that are almost too lifelike for comfort!

This book uses both natural and artificial ingredients and materials in simple yet effective ways, some of them modern, some of them in the time-honoured tradition of wreath- and garland-making.

The secret of attractive and effective floral decorations is to keep the colours unified and the form simple, and also to make sure that the style of the arrangement is in keeping with the setting proposed for it. A major element that often gets overlooked in the design of any arrangement is texture, contrasts of which give any floral decoration far greater interest and depth, so try to make sure that you consider this quality along with the colour and shape.

LEFT *The seedheads of grasses offer a rich mixture of colours, forms and textures in subtle shades of green, bronze and gold. Natural arrangements in a simple vase are ideal for such elegant and delicate ingredients.*

GOOD PRACTICE

Most of the projects in this book are very easy; very few take more than half an hour, if that, to make. No matter how simple they are, it is important to ensure that they have a professional finish and to this end you need to make them carefully, using tried and tested floristry techniques. I have included some basic techniques so that you can go about the construction in an efficient and workmanlike manner.

From past experience, I know that it pays to clear a large table to work on and to assemble all the materials and ingredients before you start. If you do, you will find it much easier to concentrate on the job in hand.

You are not obliged to follow the ideas in this book slavishly. If you cannot find one of the ingredients, then improvise with something similar. Most of the time, I offer alternative ideas for projects, and a choice of ingredients. It pays, however, to make sure that the substitutes have similar properties to those suggested: if I suggest a small-leaved plant, such as box, then use substitute leaves of a similar scale and type. Proportions, texture and form are very important in making floral displays and you ignore these at your peril.

SEASONAL PLEASURES

Where you can find fresh material from the garden or hedgerow, use it. Nothing is quite as pleasurable as being able to bring the current crop of berries, new foliage, or the season's flowers into the house to enjoy. Look for unusual ingredients, not just the ones suggested in this book. If you come across a really beautiful bunch of berries, then simply cut them and suspend them from a hook on the ceiling with a handsome ribbon. If you have too small a quantity of any ingredient in your garden to make a project of the size suggested, then simply scale down the whole concept, and display it in a suitable space. Instead of a large berry wreath, make a

OPPOSITE *The large white spire of berries from a dracaena can be hung up as a feature.*
TOP *Colourful pyracantha berries are ideal for small wreaths.*
ABOVE *Small hawthorn berries are ideal for a range of decorative displays.*

BELOW *Even something as simple as a handsome hand-carved wooden bowl of mixed pine cones can make a striking feature, either on the hearth in front of an empty fireplace in summer, or on a coffee table in front of the fireplace in autumn and winter.*

OPPOSITE *Equally striking are the rich and varied shapes and colours of gourds, which can be similarly displayed.*

tiny one that you can hang from a cupboard door, Shaker style, with a pretty ribbon. Small decorative elements, such as raffia, parcel twine and attractive tartan ribbons will all help to give the projects a professional finish and, if you are tying bows, make sure you do it the proper way (see page 21).

Autumn and winter are the ideal time to make some of these creations. There is a wealth of material out there in the garden, hedges and fields, and many celebrations that cry out for household decoration, from Thanksgiving, Halloween and Christmas, through to New Year and Valentine's day.

TECHNIQUES

Just a few basic techniques are applied to many different styles of project. This section explains some of the commonly used ones, and also suggests a range of basic equipment that comes in handy for various types of arrangement. The techniques cover those for fresh, dried and artificial flowers, as well as some useful all-purpose techniques, such as making hooks for hanging displays and creating neatly tied bows for a variety of arrangements.

LEFT *Artificial, along with fresh, berries and flowers will often need to be trimmed to size and individual sprigs can be removed from larger bunches for smaller decorations.*

equipment

You need very little in the way of equipment for most floral decorating. The basic tools and equipment are shown below but your stock will depend, in part, on the kind of ideas that you want to create and the materials you are using. If you are using fresh materials, you will need a sharp pair of secateurs to snip shrubby stems and branches and a good pair of gardening scissors for more sappy stems. You will probably need some wet oasis – a spongelike material that absorbs several times its own weight in water, into which the stems of fresh flowers can be inserted, simultaneously providing

RIGHT *The equipment shown here provides a basic range of useful tools and materials for the range of projects shown in this book. When using sprays or glues, make sure you work in a well-ventilated space and that you follow the manufacturer's instructions.*

Reading in columns, from top to bottom, left to right:
FIRST COLUMN: wreath base, florist's sticky tape (shown within the base), pliers, strong garden scissors, sharp knife
SECOND COLUMN: string, garden wire, lengths of medium-gauge florist's wire, reel wire, assorted ribbon
THIRD COLUMN: chicken wire, adhesive spray, glue gun
FOURTH COLUMN: small wooden picks, sticky putty
FIFTH COLUMN: florist's wet oasis, florist's dry oasis

moisture and appropriate support. You will need various gauges of wire, depending on the strength of the stems, when working with dried flowers. Very fine wire is used for delicate work and much thicker, tougher wire for the 'building' jobs. Useful standbys are fine reel wire for most fairly delicate tasks and multi-purpose strong green garden wire. Dry oasis is useful for keeping dried and artificial flowers in place. It is also useful to keep a selection of cords, string and ribbons in a workbox and it pays to have some sticky tape for fixing the oasis to the base of the arrangement. For artificial flowers you will need a stout pair of pliers to trim away surplus leaves. For many arrangements, a glue gun is invaluable. They are quite expensive, but work very efficiently, delivering hot glue to the exact spot required, avoiding a great deal of mess.

FRESH FLOWERS

Fresh flowers will last much longer if you condition them before use. Most flowers with hollow stems (such as tulips) bought in polythene wrapping need to be left in it in a bucket of fresh cold water for at least an hour. This enables the stems to refill with water. Any fresh flowers, however, are best left to take a long drink in a cool place for a couple of hours before being used in an arrangement. Waxy stems that are likely to seal up are best trimmed off to prevent any airlocks occurring in the stem.

1 Bought flowers (tulips in particular) should always be conditioned before using them for arrangements. Stand them, still wrapped, in a bucket of cold water for an hour or so.

2 Always remove the lower leaves so that they do not taint the water.

3 Cut off the last couple of centimetres off the base of hollow stems, to prevent airlocks. Flowers with tough, woody stems should have the last couple of centimetres crushed with a hammer.

ARTIFICIAL FLOWERS

Artificial flowers are often bought in quite large sprays, whether these are flowers, foliage or berries. They are not cheap to buy, so it makes sense to get the most out of a single spray. You can cut these down, trimming off shoots and leaves, to suit the size and nature of the project you are making. As they have a fairly tough construction, you will probably need to use a pair of pliers to cut them. I find that the foliage on artificial flowers is often a giveaway and looks less realistic. The solution is to trim it off.

trimming flowers

1 Remove individual sprigs of flowers from the main stem to make smaller projects. Pliers will be needed for thicker stems.

trimming leaves

2 The artificial flower complete with unattractive coarse and wrinkled foliage.

3 Remove any unattractive leaves, clipping them off close to the base of the stem.

1

WREATH AND GARLAND BASES

You can either make your own wreath bases (as shown in some of the projects; there is a vine base on page 30 and a wire base on page 49). Alternatively, for larger, stronger wreaths and garlands, you can either use a ready-made base or bases, which you bind with moss using reel wire, or you can make your own using chicken (turkey) wire (see below).

making your own wreath or garland base

You will need to assemble enough chicken (turkey) wire to create the base. It should be roughly 5cm (2in) longer than the proposed length and twice as wide, as you will need to double it over widthwise. Cut the wire to the appropriate size using florist's scissors (take care not to cut yourself on the sharp, cut ends). Once you have made the base, you can either turn the ends under to make a rectangular base for a garland or shape the base into a circle for a wreath, overlapping the ends of the wire.

1 Smooth out the chicken wire to form a flat base, taking care not to cut yourself on any sharp cut edges.

2 Lay the moss in the centre of the base along its length.

3 Roll the wire over the moss and bend the edges inwards so that no sharp edges protrude.

4 You can now pin whatever foliage you wish to use to the base itself. To do so, make small 'hairpins' out of medium-gauge wire by snipping off a 15cm (6in) length and bending it in half. Push the pins through the foliage, into the base itself, to secure them.

2

3

4

WIRING

Wiring flowers and foliage is usually a two-stage process. The first part is to wire several stems of flowers or foliage together to form a bunch, and the second part is to fix the bunch to the base that supports it. Fruit and nuts are normally wired in a one-stage process with stiffer wire.

wiring a bunch

1 To wire a bunch of flowers, place a piece of medium-gauge garden wire (15cm/6in long) across the stems, with one longer end, and wrap the wire a couple of times around the stems.

2 Twist the wires over the stems, and allow the longest end to protrude below the base of the stems so that it can be used to anchor the bunch to the arrangement.

wiring fruit

Individual fruits are often wired to a base; the object is to make sure it sits firmly on the base itself, so you wire across the base of spherical objects or around the base of more complex ones like cones. You will need medium-gauge wire.

3 Push a 25cm (10in) wire through the bottom third of the fruit, bend the two ends of the wire around the base of the fruit, and then twist them together to make a long firm stem which can be pushed into the base of the project.

GLUEING

A glue gun is a useful means of securing small items, such as little berries, to an arrangement. The glue, contained in sticks, is heated and delivered via the nozzle on the gun directly where it is needed, avoiding any mess.

4 Dab a tiny spot of glue on the object to be fixed.

HANGING DISPLAYS

For any hanging arrangement or display you will need to create a sturdy hook from which to hang the project. This is usually done with heavy-duty florist's wire. A loop is made by twisting the wire, hidden at the back of the project. If you want to make a decorative feature of the hanging mechanism, you can use coloured ribbon, string or raffia, or, for lightweight projects, strong button thread.

making a hook

Use medium-gauge garden wire or heavy-duty florist's wire. The gauge of the wire will be determined by the size and weight of the project. Make sure the wire you use is strong enough to support it.

1 Using strong florist's scissors or wire cutters, snip off a short length of wire, roughly 15cm (6in) long. Push the wire through the top of the project from front to back.

2 Twist the wire together two or three times to secure, close to the surface of the project.

3 Make a loop and then twist the ends of the wire firmly over each other to secure.

4 A small basket of flowers hanging from a drying rack in the kitchen, using a simple wire hook.

making bows

A good professional finish to any project you make is important. If you use ribbons for decoration, make sure that you tie any bows professionally. Florists traditionally use fancy bows, some of which are complex to make. A four-looped bow looks smart, and is useful for projects of various sizes. The instructions here show you how to make one. You will need a length of ribbon roughly 10 times as long as the length of the loops. Use one hand to hold the loops in place as you make them and the other to fold the ribbon over to form the four loops.

1 Measuring in roughly 10cm (4in) from one end of the ribbon, make a single loop in it. Hold it in place with one thumb.

2 Make the opposite loop by doubling the ribbon back over itself. Hold it again with the thumb.

3 Then form the third loop by taking the ribbon over in the same direction as the first loop, but behind it. Then make the fourth loop as you did the second loop.

4 Finally hold all four loops in one hand and, with a small piece of wire, fasten the centre of the ribbon.

5 Cut the ends off neatly a few centimetres below the loops.

FRESH
DISPLAYS

There is a wealth of plants to choose from for fresh displays, not forgetting foliage and berries as well as flowers. If you use those that dry or last well, your displays will stay looking good for several weeks or even months. It pays to be creative about the style of the decoration, too, and where you position it. Different kinds of foliage and berries make attractive wall hangings, but you can also use the same construction principle to surround a platter of fruit on the dinner table or encircle a chandelier.

LEFT *A little wreath made solely from pyracantha berries, wired in bunches to a simple base. It looks most effective if the berries are packed closely, and it can be used fresh and then allowed to dry.*

fresh ingredients

While most of us are familiar with the popular florist's flowers, we tend to ignore the fact that our own gardens, and those of our friends, can provide us with a great deal of useful material for flower displays, either to flesh out small bunches of expensive bought flowers or as attractive arrangements in their own right.

Among the best ingredients to be found are the wonderful array of seedheads and small fruits that can be gleaned from gardens and hedgerows in late summer and early autumn. Many of these dry well and will provide attractive colour in the house for many months in winter, when there is little else to choose from. Among my favourites (and very popular with birds, too, so you need to hurry to get yours first!) are the hips of different roses. They vary greatly in size and colour, some as

big as cherry tomatoes, others tiny and delicate. You can use them to decorate wreaths and garlands, and they look particularly effective when combined with birch twigs to make a Scandinavian style wreath (see page 32). Pyracantha berries are another very valuable stand by, and they come in shades of gold, orange and yellow, depending on the variety grown. I like to use these to make small wreaths or mini-tree decorations (see pages 76-7).

Evergreen leaves are another extremely valuable stand-by. Different leaf forms are good for particular purposes. The soft, largish deep green leaves of ivy last well and are ideal for covering the base of a wreath or garland. Tough glossy oval leaves of magnolia or camellia will make a wreath or garland base in their own right. Smaller, more bushy leaves can be used to flesh out a flowering display – small sprigs of privet, for example, look good against the slender stems of florists' carnations. Aromatic leaves, such as those of sage, bay, lavender or rosemary, make wonderful scented wreaths which dry well.

LEFT *Rosehips, crab apples and pyracantha and holly berries are just some of the fruits available in autumn.*
THIS PAGE *Evergreen foliage, from top left clockwise: sarcococca, bay, thuja, camellia, ivy, choisya, holly (two types) and box.*

shaker-style cranberry heart

Sometimes very small and simple decorations can be even more effective and eye-catching than much more elaborate ones. This classic Shaker-style heart, made from either fresh or dried cranberries strung on florist's wire, makes an attractive decoration for a kitchen cupboard or dresser. The wire should be fairly fine but strong enough to be pushed through the fruit without buckling.

Different shapes and forms can be tried out and various materials used with equally attractive results. Bright scarlet chilli peppers look great and you can thread them alternately with bay leaves if you wish. Blueberries and other small round fruit, as well as large berries of different descriptions, are good for this kind of decoration too. All these ingredients look good fresh, but are equally attractive when dry.

If you hang the decoration from a ribbon, try to ensure that the colour and pattern are chosen to complement the style and character of the little decoration. Narrow gingham ribbons always look fresh and cheerful. A blue and white one would look good with the blueberries, and a green and white with the chilli peppers and bay leaves. If you wish, you can add a simple straight wire, threaded with cranberries, from which to hang the heart. Attach a simple bow at the join, and at the top of the long string or make a fancy bow (see page 21).

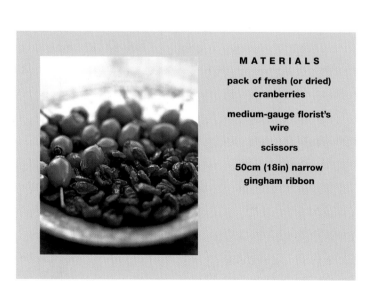

MATERIALS

pack of fresh (or dried) cranberries

medium-gauge florist's wire

scissors

50cm (18in) narrow gingham ribbon

how to make

These are just about the simplest decorations to make. If you have children, they might well enjoy helping you or making their own.

1 Thread the cranberries onto the florist's wire, pushing the wire through the centre of each cranberry. Push the cranberries close together, as you thread them onto the wire. When you have threaded a sufficient length of wire, bend the wired cranberries into a circle, twist the ends over at the top and snip off the wire.

2 Push the top of the circle inwards to form a rough heart shape. Finally, create a small wire loop on the back of the heart.

sage and rosehip wreath

This aromatic wreath can be made and enjoyed fresh and then left to dry. The principal ingredients are purple-leaved sage (*Salvia officinalis* 'Purpurascens') decorated with rosehips. The wreath will reduce in size slightly when dry and the leaves will crinkle, but the overall effect is still extremely attractive. Rose leaves and hips (from the bluish-grey leaved rose known as *Rosa glauca*) have been added for decoration, but any brightly coloured berries can be used in their place. Indeed, you are not obliged to use sage leaves – there are plenty of others in the garden to choose from. Bay (*Laurus nobilis)*, for example, will produce a similarly attractive dense shape with its glossy evergreen leaves that are comparable in size to those of sage and equally aromatic. Box (*Buxus sempervirens*) could be used instead and will create a much more densely packed appearance. Both of the latter plants dry well.

The base for this particular wreath is constructed from a few lengths of vine and is one of the simplest to make, producing a very pleasing, natural, slightly asymmetrical effect. If you prefer a more classic wreath shape, then you can bind the leaves to a traditional wire wreath frame, filled with moss.

Similarly simple wreaths can be made with other ingredients: an all berry wreath made of densely packed pyracantha berries will look equally good both fresh and dried (see overleaf). Even seedheads can be used, tightly packed in small bunches so that they completely cover the base.

ABOVE *The dark velvety foliage of the purple sage (*Salvia officinalis *'Purpurascens').*
LEFT *Decorated with rosehips, sage makes an aromatic wreath that can be used fresh or dried.*

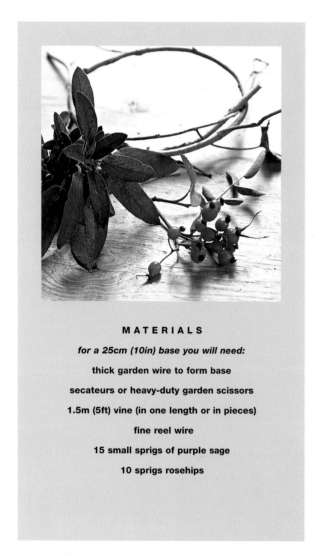

MATERIALS

for a 25cm (10in) base you will need:

thick garden wire to form base

secateurs or heavy-duty garden scissors

1.5m (5ft) vine (in one length or in pieces)

fine reel wire

15 small sprigs of purple sage

10 sprigs rosehips

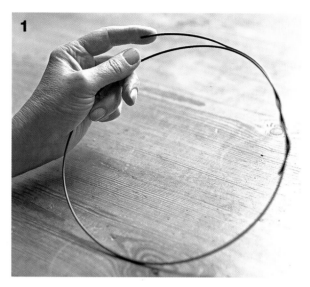

how to make

You will first have to make the base from thick garden wire, then attach the vines to create a fuller circle. To this the sage leaves are added and, when these cover the wreath, you can add the sprigs of rosehips for decoration.

1 Cut a length of garden wire roughly 15cm (6in) longer than the intended radius of the wreath and twist the ends over to close the circle.

2 Attach the length or lengths of vine to the base using fine reel wire.

3 Attach the first sprig of sage to the base, using fine reel wire, binding it over the stems two or three times to secure. Do not cut off the wire.

4

5

4 Continue to add the sprigs, overlapping them slightly, stems to tips, and binding them with wire until the circle is covered. Snip off the wire.

5 Push the stems of the rosehips through the leaves at evenly spaced intervals around the wreath. (If using berries with softer stems, you will need to wire them first, see page 18.)

BERRY WREATH ALTERNATIVE

A wreath made entirely of pyracantha berries creates a very different effect. Choose the materials from whatever is available in the garden using the ideas suggested on page 29. Different forms and varieties will be available in various regions: simply choose the best of what you can find. The construction is exactly the same as for the sage wreath: individual bunches of berries are wired to the wreath and closely packed for the best effect.

swedish candelabra

Simple but attractive decoration can be added to an existing candelabra to give it a more festive air. Among the most suitable materials for this kind of decoration are plants with long, slender, slightly flexible shoots that will bend easily. For the project shown here, shoots of climbing roses, complete with hips, were used and for the alternative, slender birch twigs. Among other successful choices would be various ivies, Russian vine or hops. Artificial stems can also be used. To create the same natural-looking effect, it would be a good idea to strip off some of the leaves to create a slightly asymmetrical appearance.

It will give the arrangement a more unified look if you match the candle colours to those of the decoration: scarlet candles for the rosehip version, green candles for the cone and twig one. With a very simple twiggy wreath, you could add small silver or gold decorations, such as silver-sprayed tiny fruit (kumquats are ideal), small cones wired to the base, plastic berries in silver or gold, added in small bunches to it, and complete the look with silver or gold candles.

The candelabra shown here is an inexpensive black iron one, but you can modify the design to suit whatever style of candelabra that you possess. When putting the decoration together, take care to ensure that none of the leaves or branches actually touch the candles themselves. In any event, no lit candles should be left unattended.

LEFT AND RIGHT *In this version of the candelabra, bright scarlet candles have been used, to match the scarlet hips. They are shown lit, left. If you use non-drip candles, you will get no unsightly and irritating blobs of wax on the display or on your furniture.*

how to make

There are several ways in which you could make this simple decoration. The one shown below creates a rough wreath shape, which you can reuse if you wish as a wall hanging (see page 46). For a less permanent arrangement, you can simply wire individual shoots to the candelabra base to make a loose, informal decoration.

1 Take three birch branches and bind the stems together at the base with reel wire.

2 Loosely bind the wire up towards the tip of the branches to pull together any wayward stems. Do not pull the wire so tight that the sideshoots are all uniformly tucked in. Small shoots should stray out at either side.

3 Take the next three stems and add them to the first three about two thirds of the way along, base to tip, wrapping them loosely with reel wire as you do so.

4 Bind the tips of the stems to the base of the first stems to make a rough circle to fit the diameter of your candelabra. Bind together to complete the circle.

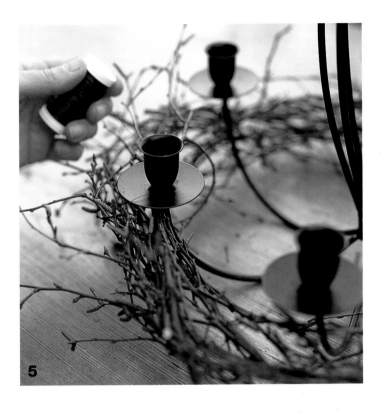

5 Add the circle of twiggy branches to the base of the candelabra, wiring it on securely at each candleholder.

6 Add the rosehips, pushing the thicker ends of the branches into the twiggy base.

CONE ALTERNATIVE

This version shows the same cast iron candelabra, but decorated this time with alder twigs, complete with small greenish-brown cones. Green candles complete the display, toning with the colours of the foliage and the cones.

35

LASTING
DISPLAYS

In addition to dried flowers, you can now find very realistic synthetic flowers, foliage and berries, giving you a range of attractive all-year-round floral decorations for the home. A traditional-looking flower arrangement for a permanent place in the hall or in a window embrasure can be created from a mixture of dried and synthetic flowers, seedheads and foliage. Slender artificial grasses, dyed in rich colours and arranged in elegant chrome containers, make a marvellous minimal decoration for a contemporary living room, too.

LEFT *A close–up detail of the surprisingly realistic small delicate waxy petals of an artificial flowering orchid, shown on page 45.*

lasting ingredients

The range of artificial flowers has grown greatly in recent years and the home flower arranger now has a wealth of really good quality materials to choose from, which are almost indistinguishable from the real thing. Such is the quality of these flowers, fruits and seedheads that they can be used alone or to flesh out a display of fresh or dried flowers.

The most important element to look out for when purchasing artificial flowers is good colour quality which matches, as closely as possible, the delicate tones and shades of the real thing. Not all artificial flowers, however, are exact copies of real plants. Some are designed to enhance the natural features of the real plants, adding new colours to the existing shade

range, for example, or introducing special effects, such as gilding or silvering. These latter items are invaluable for creating a touch of glamour in festive displays.

I find that the most effective are the sprays of flowers and berries which can be trimmed down and used as small sprigs in other arrangements, but I also like the strong impact that a bunch of artificial tulips or orchid stems (see page 45) can make. I tend to keep a special place in the house for permanent displays of artificial flowers. On a table by a large sunny window, I have a permanent display of soft tones of pink, mauve and green, composed of artificial hydrangea heads, poppies and cabbage roses, which I flesh out with real but preserved leaves. In a sunny position, real flowers droop quickly and dried flowers fade, but the artificial ones keep going throughout every season, always looking as good as new.

LEFT *Just a few of the wide range of artificial berries and fruits that can now be bought from craft shops.*
THIS PAGE *Flowers can be very realistic-looking. Those shown here are lilies, dill and carnations with grass seedheads and beech and eucalyptus leaves.*

grasses and seedheads

For a modern setting, simple, slender vases in monochromatic materials, such as plain white or black ceramics, iron, aluminium or steel, can be filled with colourful stems or grasses, either artificial or real. Equally useful are the seedheads of a range of different plants, their ghostly outlines ideal for creating an extremely effective minimalist decoration that relies on its sculptural qualities for effect.

To achieve the right look, you need to match the shape, colour and form of the container to that of the ingredients it contains. Simplicity is the keynote. You could use wonderfully contorted twigs of hazel (*Corylus avellana* 'Contorta'), slender golden willow branches or bright scarlet dogwood stems, or an artificial version of any of these, in tall, elegant containers made of steel or chrome. A natural bamboo container would be perfect for delicate branches of pussy willow with its fluffy catkins.

Tall, slender decorations look their best when employed in symmetrical pairs, to flank a particular setting: either side of a fireplace or doorway, for example. Ideally, the vases and their ingredients should not be dwarfed by the setting, and the height of the whole decoration should retain some balance between the container and its contents. The general rule in flower arranging is one of thirds: the container is normally one third of the overall height of the arrangement, but with tall, shapely arrangements, a half and half rule seems to work more effectively.

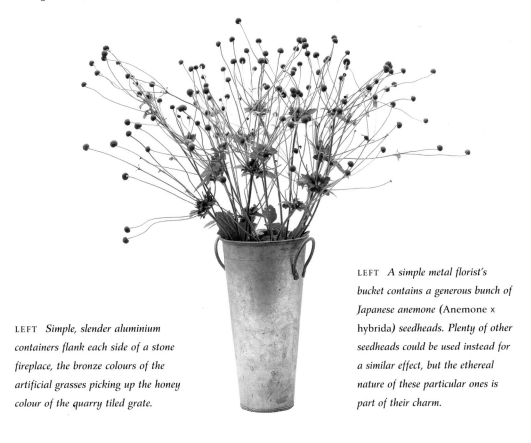

LEFT *Simple, slender aluminium containers flank each side of a stone fireplace, the bronze colours of the artificial grasses picking up the honey colour of the quarry tiled grate.*

LEFT *A simple metal florist's bucket contains a generous bunch of Japanese anemone (Anemone x hybrida) seedheads. Plenty of other seedheads could be used instead for a similar effect, but the ethereal nature of these particular ones is part of their charm.*

41

lasting flower arrangement

This simple arrangement in silver, green and gold is made from fresh, dried and artificial flowers, but the fresh ones will dry in the arrangement so that it will keep for many months. You can follow the same principle of construction for a range of flower arrangements. The principal aim is to create a good balanced structure out of elegant foliage plants with interesting leaves, which provides the frame to which the flowers are added. It pays to keep the colour theme simple. Using one or at the most two toning colours adds to the impact of the arrangement.

When choosing a container, pick one that is roughly one third of the height of the final arrangement. It needs an inverted triangular shape so that the flowers fan out slightly in the arrangement. A plain ceramic or terracotta vase looks attractive and does not detract from the effect made by the flowers.

Arrangements that rely on seedheads are best positioned against the light – on a window ledge or table in front of a window so that their ethereal qualities are best appreciated. Texture is an important element in any flower arrangement, so it pays to use plant material (dried or artificial) with a variety of textural qualities: glossy or matt, smooth or spiky, soft or hard. Similarly look for contrasts in the form of the flowers: contrast those with simple large papery petals with those with small florets to add variety to the display.

RIGHT *This delicate arrangement is beautifully balanced, the dark foliage setting off the more ethereal flowers and seedheads to perfection.*

MATERIALS

wet oasis

container

beech leaves

lavender

achillea

eucalyptus leaves

lizianthus

alliums

golden hops

anemone seedheads

1

2

how to make

This flower arrangement uses wet oasis but the flowers will then dry out to form a lasting arrangement. Cut the oasis to roughly fit the container with a little to spare at the top. Strip the lower leaves from the stems and hold against the vase, resting on the table, to judge the appropriate length required.

1 Make sure the oasis fits into the container so that the top protrudes about 2.5cm (1in) above the rim. Then insert a framing structure made out of beech leaves.

2 Add stems of lavender between the beech leaves, taking care to create a balanced shape.

3 You can then add the achillea flowers to the arrangement, which will bulk it out considerably. Then add the eucalyptus leaves.

4 Fill in with the remaining ingredients except the anemone seedheads. Finish off by adding a few anemone seedheads to fill any spaces.

3

4

ORCHID ALTERNATIVE

A similarly tall arrangement can be made with architectural artificial flowers. Buy a few stems of orchids, attach them to cane stakes with moss and raffia, and insert them into a block of oasis wedged into an attractive container. Cover the oasis with moss to disguise it.

laurel garland

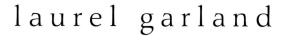

Simple and elegant, this laurel garland, and its wreath alternative shown overleaf, are extremely easy to make and have a splendidly classical appeal, which nevertheless works just as well in minimalist city apartments. You can use both the garland and the wreath bases for other decorations, hanging bunches of berries, ribbons or hearts, to dangle in the centre of the wreath or from the points of the garland, if you wish.

Simple but effective, garlands and wreaths can be constructed from any large, shiny evergreen leaves, like those of laurel (*Prunus lusitanicus*), which are strong and durable as well as having a glossy sheen. Among the evergreen bushes and shrubs suitable for this kind of simple garland are camellias and bay, and evergreen magnolia, such as *Magnolia grandiflora,* and evergreen viburnums, such as *Viburnum tinus lauristinus*. Stitched together with tough thread or fine wire, and backed by a circle of heavy-duty garden wire in the case of the wreath, they are ideally suited to modern, fairly minimal interiors where plain colours and simple shapes predominate.

You will need sufficient sprigs of greenery to enable you to strip off enough evenly sized leaves for the length you require. About a dozen 25cm (10in) long sprigs would be enough for a 90cm (36in) long garland. It is important to pick similarly sized and shaped leaves to ensure a balanced symmetrical appearance. Once you have mastered the technique of stitching the leaves together, you can decide what form you want the decoration to take, but your decision will inevitably be governed by the setting. If you want to decorate a mantelpiece or shelf, then a garland is the obvious answer. The wreath looks good on a chimney breast, plain kitchen wall or a door. To give the wreath impact, you can hang a little bunch of berries from the top. In the case of the garland, similar decorations could be suspended from the points of any loops you create.

You can, of course, make these simple projects from artificial leaves instead, but they tend to lack the sheen of natural ones and are usually best suited to more elaborate decorations. However, if you sprayed the leaves silver or gold, they would make an attractive party or Christmas decoration, hung perhaps with a bunch or bunches of small silver cones, tied on with metallic ribbon.

LEFT *A laurel garland frames an old range, looped attractively to fit the fireplace surround. Above hangs the birch wreath used to decorate the candelabra on page 32.*

MATERIALS

several sprigs of laurel

scissors

darning needle

button thread or fine florist's wire

several sprigs of crab apple (if you wish to decorate the garland or wreath)

how to make

The length of the garland is normally dictated by the setting. For a garland to suit most mantelpieces, you would need a length of about 2.1m (8ft). If you wish, hang small decorative bunches or circles of crab apples from the apex of each loop in the garland.

1 Strip the leaves from the sprigs of laurel, and select those that match one another in size and shape. Be careful to snip the stalk off completely from the base of each leaf.

2 Overlapping the leaves tail to top by 2cm (½in) as shown, insert the needle and thread from the underside through to the top side of the leaves, penetrating both.

3 Make a neat stitch across the vein of the leaf, as shown, inserting the needle through to the back of the leaves before repeating step 2 for the next pair of leaves. Continue in this way until a sufficient length has been made.

WREATH ALTERNATIVE

To make a laurel wreath, after step 3 join the last leaf to the first to make a complete circle. Cut a length of heavy-duty wire to the circumference of the wreath, bind the ends to make a circle, and then bind the leaf wreath to the wire using fine wire. Decorate with a small circle of crab apples threaded onto fine wire (see page 26), suspended from the wire base, and hang the wreath on a plain wall (below) for the best effect.

TABLE DISPLAYS

Smaller displays, made in the round, are ideal for table centres or for small side or bedside tables. Fresh, dried or artificial flowers and plant material can be used to great effect. Smaller flowers and leaves are ideal for these kinds of arrangements, as are those built around a central candle, which casts a romantic light over a supper table, for example. Always take care when using candles to ensure that they are never left unattended when lit. Non-drip candles are ideal as they create less mess than ordinary ones.

LEFT *This large table centre composed of artificial and dried flowers, foliage and berries, in a toning mixture of colours, can stay in place more or less permanently apart from the need every few months to remove any dust.*

spring table centre

If you want to make a spring table centre for an Easter celebration, for example, then a small mossy nest filled with eggs and decorated with spring flowers is ideal. You can vary the size of the project to suit the position in which you want to display it. I made this one in a 23cm (8in) diameter metal flan tin, but you could use any shallow dish or tray that you happen to have available.

The mossy decoration is made using flat moss that is bound to the tin (or, in the case of a cardboard shape, glued to it) using garden string or raffia. The little violas in this version were pot grown and then arranged around the inside of the tin. The centre is covered with garden moss and then filled with quails' eggs. If you prefer, you could fill the entire centre with chocolate eggs as a party treat for children.

Any small flowers could be substituted for the violas. Small primroses would look good, as would grape hyacinths. You need to ensure that the height of the tin, however, is sufficient to mask the compost in which the plants are grown. If you mist the whole project with water regularly, it should stay looking fresh for a couple of weeks, provided the house is not too hot. Do not put it in very bright sunlight, however, or in deep shade, if you want it to last.

LEFT *This little nest of eggs, bordered with flowers, makes a pretty addition to an Easter-time dinner table, but you could change the flowers (using similarly small pot-grown plants) around the outside of the arrangement, to create a more or less permanent centrepiece.*

MATERIALS

23cm (8in) flan tin

fresh moss

garden twine

scissors

6 viola plants

6 quails' eggs (or foil-wrapped chocolate eggs)

how to make

You simply need to wrap moss around a shallow tin before filling it with the ingredients suggested.

1 Bind the sides of a shallow flan tin with the moss, tying it round the centre with garden twine to hold it in place.

2 Then trim any surplus moss from the top and base of the tin.

3 Pack the edge of the tin with the flowers.

4 Cover the centre with moss and fill with quails' or chocolate eggs.

winter berry candle pots

This simple decoration makes an ideal table centre for an informal supper party, for example, or a pair of them could be used to flank either end of a bookcase or mantelpiece. The ingredients are fresh, but will dry well to make a lasting arrangement. You can make simpler alternatives out of a single ingredient, demonstrated by the ivy berry basket shown below. If you decide to make the arrangement using artificial or dried ingredients, you can swap the pre-soaked wet oasis for dry oasis. Otherwise the method is the same.

I used a small straight-sided terracotta pot for this arrangement because I think its rustic simplicity suits the style of the foliage and berries, and complements their soft autumnal colours. It is important when making these kind of decorations, where the pot itself is a major part of the arrangement, that the texture, style and colour of the container harmonize well with the ingredients.

As a useful professional tip, it pays to remember to make the oasis slightly taller (by a couple of centimetres) than the pot containing it, so that you can insert the flower material into the sides as well as into the top of the oasis, to cover it. Make sure that you never leave lit candles unattended.

RIGHT *This little candle pot makes an attractive pool of light either in the centre of a small table or on any available flat surface.*

IVY BERRY ALTERNATIVE

In this simple version of the candle pot the same tall church candle is set in the centre, this time in a small wire basket, surrounded with creamy berries and deep green foliage of tree ivy, which set off the candle to perfection. If you wish, you can make individual versions for place settings. Use saucers, fixing shorter candles to them with florist's tape and surrounding them similarly with ivy leaves and berries.

MATERIALS

plastic liner

scissors

terracotta pot

wet oasis

cocktail sticks

15cm (6in) church candle

florist's tape

tree ivy leaves and berries

sprigs of pittosporum

sprigs of skimmia berries

sprigs of hypericum berries

acorns

how to make

1 Cut a suitably sized piece of plastic liner and insert it into the pot to line the sides. Then cut a square of wet oasis, pre-soaked, just tall enough to rise above the rim of the pot by 5cm (2in).

2 Wrap three pairs of cocktail sticks to the base of the candle, and bind them with florist's tape. Then insert the base of the candle into the top of the oasis.

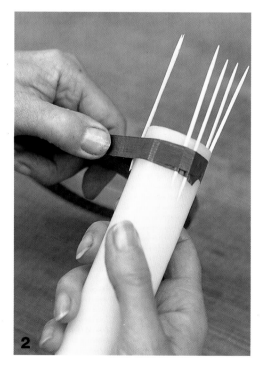

3 Insert a few tree ivy leaves into the sides and top of the oasis, making sure that a good few centimetres of candle are left clear of the foliage.

4 Snip small sprigs of pittosporum and skimmia berries, and then insert them into the spaces between the tree ivy leaves. Add a few sprigs of hypericum berries.

5 Lastly, add some tree ivy berries and a couple of acorns or any other small nuts, such as cobnuts, as a finishing touch.

artificial flower
table centres

I like to see the table with some floral decoration; it looks undressed without it. The great advantage of artificial flowers is their lasting quality, but you would not want to look at the same arrangement day in, day out so it is a good idea to make up several small arrangements and alternate them, according to the mood, the occasion and the style of the table setting.

Some of my favourites are very small – ideal for an intimate supper or a breakfast table, for example. The containers in which they are displayed are a vital part of the whole design, so it pays to choose them carefully, ensuring that their style, colour, shape and texture match those of the flowers they contain. Why not make up a few very small displays in miniature containers, such as coffee cups or egg cups? They could contain exquisite little displays, like the tiny snowdrops nestling in a bed of small ivy leaves and fresh green garden moss (which you need to spray with water and change periodically, as it will turn brown in time otherwise), shown overleaf. Tiny jewel-like flowers, such as pansies, violets or narcissus, are also ideal for this purpose. Small terracotta pots filled with massed heads of lavender, tied with a simple paper ribbon bow, would look good too.

A summery arrangement of bright pinks and small roses, in an old-fashioned patterned china container, makes an excellent choice for an evening party. Bright yellow carnations and small lilies, backed with strong green leaves (shown overleaf), create a younger, fresher, less formal look for casual supper parties.

Most of these small arrangements can be arranged using a block of dry florist's oasis wedged into the neck of the container. It will hold the stems firmly in place, allowing you to position the stems exactly where you want them (see page 15).

When you make up a table centre, it is a good idea to construct it using a lazy Susan (a revolving platter), so that you can keep turning the arrangement as you make it, ensuring it looks good when seen from all sides.

LEFT *A pretty little table centre has been arranged in a delicate pink-patterned china bowl. It is composed of artificial carnations, rosebuds, foliage and berries in matching shades of pink.*

Larger centrepieces are best designed symmetrically with the tallest flowers in the centre, graduating down to the rim of the container on all sides. You can ring the changes both in terms of the size and the nature of the display, depending on the situation for which it is intended.

For a traditional display, a large shallow bowl, filled to the brim with toning flowers, berries and foliage in soft shades of pinks and mauves, echoes the glorious relaxed profusion of garden roses in summer (below centre). If you keep the design loose and simple, and ensure that you use only harmonizing tones (similar depths or shades of colours so that no colour in particular leaps out from the others) you can combine any flowers and foliage that you like. Avoid white at all costs, as it tends to catch the eye and break up the unity of the design.

On a more modern note, you can use simple containers with clean lines and display just a few flowers in them. These kind of arrangements work well in contemporary homes on a simple wooden table, for example. Use either fresh or synthetic flowers, but keep the colour palette limited in range. Include one or two large flowers, such as lilies or roses, to help to anchor the arrangement.

BELOW LEFT *A couple of artificial snowdrops, set in moss and ivy, create a tiny, pretty display in a china coffee cup.*
BELOW CENTRE *In complete contrast, this glorious table centre of artificial and dried flowers in warm, toning shades makes an excellent permanent centrepiece. Use big artificial and dried blooms, such as poppies and hydrangeas, to provide the structure and fill out the arrangement with berries, seedheads, foliage and smaller flowers to form a domed shape.*
RIGHT AND BELOW RIGHT *For smaller displays in a modern setting, informal arrangements with a simple colour theme look fresh and clean.*

FESTIVE DISPLAYS

Special occasions deserve special treatments. Whether for seasonal celebrations, such as Thanksgiving, Christmas or Easter, or for parties, it is worth spending extra time and effort to mark the occasion with an attractive arrangement – be it a garland, wreath, table centre display or a little festive tree. All kinds of different material can be used as decoration: real or synthetic, fresh or dried, naturally coloured, dyed or sprayed with gold or silver. Creating an unusual and eye-catching display adds a touch of glamour to any important event.

LEFT *This winter wreath, composed of holly, ivy, alder twigs and pine cones, has been made on a traditional wreath base (see page 71).*

winter mantelpiece

For a special winter party or seasonal celebration such as Christmas, why not decorate the mantelpiece to create a special welcome? Because the shelf is already there to support the arrangement, you do not have to spend time creating a garland for these long displays. Simply use the foliage in sprigs and position them where you wish.

Candles create a wonderfully soft and romantic light but obviously you need to ensure that they are not left unattended once they are lit! Make sure, too, that any combustible plant material is placed far enough away from the flame. The short, fat white candles are useful because they are very stable and take a long time to burn down.

During winter, you can make use of wonderful cones, such as large and small pine and alder cones, and also of seasonally available fruit, such as tangerines, apples and oranges.

The best effects are created when the arrangement is not too carefully or symmetrically placed. Compose small groups of ingredients – cones, fruit and candles – among foliage (either artificial or real).

You can mix artificial and real ingredients quite successfully in these kinds of display, using perhaps a mixture of fresh foliage from the garden with artificial berries or, equally, a synthetic foliage garland with fresh fruit and cones.

LEFT AND RIGHT
A mantelpiece decoration gives the house a special glow at Christmas using a simple, informal grouping of cones, fruit, holly and ivy leaves and candles along the length of a stone mantelpiece.

MATERIALS

ivy leaves

medium-gauge wire

secateurs

large pine cones

small pine cones

variegated holly

lotus flower seedheads

oranges

artificial apple rings

beeswax candles, varying heights

how to make

You can create a foliage garland by binding together lengths of ivy, either real or artificial.

1 Overlap the ends of each length of ivy and wire them together using medium-gauge wire.

2 Position the garland and decorate with groups of fruit, cones, foliage and candles.

HARVEST HOME ALTERNATIVES

For a simpler effect (above), in Swedish style, use small coloured candles, artificial fruit slices and a few sprigs of evergreen foliage. The same decorative principle has been used to create a sumptuous, mantelpiece garland, made from ivy leaves (below). Large heads of dried hydrangea flowers and different synthetic berries replace the cones. Seasonal fruits, such as apples or oranges, complete the Renaissance-style decoration.

harvest wreath

A wreath hanging on a door makes an attractive welcome for any party or festivity. If you do not have access to natural ingredients, you can use artificial ones very successfully to produce highly naturalistic effects. You need to select the artificial material carefully, choosing toning or matching colours, and you will need to 'doctor' it to make it easier to work with. Many of the artificial ingredients, while attractive in themselves, look 'clumpy' unless you strip away some of the leaves, berries or flowers. You can do this quite easily using scissors for the lighterweight materials, and a pair of pliers for the tougher forms (see page 17).

This particular wreath has been made from an ivy stem base, but you could equally easily make one from another creeper, such as wisteria (see page 30). You can decorate the wreath with a mixture of berries and flowers, choosing colours appropriate for your decorative scheme. In this case, the colours chosen are softly toning mauves and greens and are ideal for both summer and autumn parties or gatherings. Choosing golds, russets and reds would give the wreath an attractive autumnal look and dark green, red and silver would give it a suitably festive wintry look. An Easter wreath could be made on an artificial ivy base, to which small 'eggs', glued into little baskets, could be wired, with a small Easter chicken dangling from a ribbon in the centre of the wreath (as the crab apple ring does from the centre of the laurel wreath, see page 49).

The wreath is made entirely of artificial and dried ingredients and will last indefinitely. You might need to shake it now and again, very gently, to remove any dust.

LEFT *Hanging on a wooden door, this autumnal-looking wreath has been made out of artificial and dried ingredients (fresh hydrangea flowers, shown in close up above) and a few fresh silver birch twigs and fresh moss.*

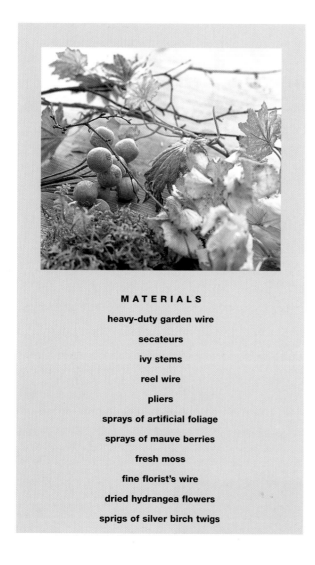

MATERIALS

heavy-duty garden wire

secateurs

ivy stems

reel wire

pliers

sprays of artificial foliage

sprays of mauve berries

fresh moss

fine florist's wire

dried hydrangea flowers

sprigs of silver birch twigs

how to make

1 Make a wreath base from heavy-duty garden wire and cover it with ivy stems (see steps 1 and 2 on page 30). This one is roughly 38cm (15in) in diameter.

2 Snip off pieces of artificial foliage using pliers and bind the pieces to the base using reel wire, ensuring that it is evenly covered. Use smaller pieces if necessary to fill any gaps.

3 Now start to add the decoration. Snip off small sprigs of berries and wrap the bases in moss, using fine florist's wire.

4 Apply these at evenly spaced intervals – roughly four to fit this size of base – and bind onto the base with wire. Trim the hydrangea flowers into several smaller sprigs, and add these sprigs in the spaces in between the berries.

5 Finally add some small sprigs of silver birch randomly around the edges of the wreath to give it a loose appearance. The stems are tough enough to be pushed into the wreath base without the need for wiring.

CHRISTMAS ALTERNATIVE

This particular wreath has been made from fresh pine sprays in a loose arrangement, fixed to a simple base (see page 30), to which holly, cones and birch twigs have been added. The finished arrangement has been sprayed with artificial frosting.

twig tree

This festive tree can be used for any special occasion – Christmas, Easter or a special birthday or anniversary. You can adapt the form and the decorations to suit the occasion. The one shown here was created for a golden wedding party. To adapt it to suit different occasions, simply add a few appropriate decorations. Some additional ideas are shown on pages 76-77. For a silver wedding, for example, you could spray the pot and the decorations silver rather than gold. At Easter time, you could replace the birds with Easter chicks and fill the baskets with small eggs. At Christmas, you could create a colour theme for the decorations – silver, red and green for example.

If you wish, you can make the tree more minimalist in appearance by simply using one kind of decoration. The tiny pomanders made from kumquats (with varying designs) look extremely effective used in this way.

The choice of twigs depends on what you can find locally, but the best ones to use tend to be dark, fairly strong and with a slightly knobbly appearance. The twigs used here came from an apple (*Malus sp*) tree. The more highly branched the twigs are, the greater the scope to hang the decorations. Whatever twigs you choose, you will need to anchor them in a stable base. Florist's dry oasis works very well, but make sure the pot is deep enough to take a reasonably large block.

Some of the decorations for this tree, such as the artificial birds and the artificial flowers in the baskets, are shop-bought from a hobby or homecraft store; others are homemade. If you wish, you can make small wreaths to hang on the tree. You can make these from whatever small fruits and berries you can find, but you could also thread small pasta shapes onto wire (soften them first by cooking them for a minute or two). The size depends on the scale of the tree, but ideally they should all be of similar size on a single project.

If you put the tree in or near the window, the gold- or silver-sprayed decorations will catch the light beautifully.

LEFT *The twig tree is hung with a mixture of decorations including mini pomanders, cones and little baskets, all in shades of gold and orange.*

73

MATERIALS

knife

dry oasis

terracotta pot

suitable twigs for the tree

pea gravel

kumquats and cloves for the pomanders

medium-gauge wire

secateurs

tartan bows

fruit rings

gold-sprayed cones, baskets and seedheads

metallic baubles

artificial birds

how to make

You need to collect four or five twiggy branches of approximately the same length – these are about 38cm (15in) tall.

1 Cut the oasis into a wedge shaped block to fit snugly inside the container.

2 Arrange the four or five twigs so that they fan out attractively.

3 Fill the container with pea gravel so that the oasis is covered. Finally hang the branches with the decorations of your choice.

making kumquat pomanders

Kumquats – small citrus fruit the colour of oranges – are ideal for making pomanders for a small festive tree. You can buy them from the supermarket during the winter and stud them with dried cloves in whatever patterns you find most attractive.

1 Assemble the fruit and the cloves with which to stud them on a work surface. It is quite a messy business so use a wipable top on which to work, or spread paper on the surface.

2 Insert the cloves in lines around the fruit, gently pushing the pointed end of the clove into the fruit. You can create a circle of cloves around the diameter of the fruit, or make a quartered pattern. Alternatively, stud the whole fruit with cloves.

3 Wire each fruit in the usual way (see page 19) using medium-gauge florist's wire.

4 Hang the fruits on the twig tree, or, if you wish, use them as decorations for a Christmas tree or garland.

OTHER FRUIT DECORATIONS

You can make all sorts of small decorations from different kinds of fruits and cones, either as mini wreaths or simply by spraying the fruit or nuts with gold or silver spray paint.

miniature berry wreaths

LEFT AND RIGHT Pyracantha berries can be wired in bunches onto a mini wreath, and a fine ribbon used to hang from the tree.

miniature dried fruit wreaths

BELOW Dried cranberries or raisins can be strung onto a short length of wire, twisted at the ends to form a ring, and decorated with a simple bow.

sprayed decorations

BELOW Various dried or artificial small decorations can be sprayed with gold paint. Shown from left to right below are gold sprayed seedheads, a little basket filled with tiny fruits or flowers and a pine cone. Hang them on the tree with fine gold ribbons.

CITRUS ALTERNATIVE

*Here a fresh pot-grown plant, in this case a small citrus tree, has been decorated for
a party by covering the surface of the pot with small cones and tying a ribbon
around the base. You could treat any attractive pot-grown plant in the same way.*

suppliers

UK

Visit your local florists and supermarkets for a good choice of inexpensive fresh flowers. Large department stores often stock a good selection of artificial and dried flowers and seedheads, trimmings, accessories and containers. Local garden centres can often supply most florist's equipment.

All Trimmings
26A Central Trading Estate
Cable Street
Wolverhampton WV2 2RJ
Tel: (01902) 451 560
www.alltrimmings.co.uk
Florist's sundries and trimmings
Mail order available

The Flower Barn
37 Hill Lane
Barnham
West Sussex PO22 0BL
Tel: (01243) 553 490
www.flowerbarn.co.uk
Silk, dried and parchment flowers,
artificial fruits and berries, sundries

Hobbycraft
Tel: (08000) 272387
www.hobbycraft.co.uk
Silk flowers and craft sundries
Stores nationwide

Lavenders of London
Unit 12, The Metro Centre
St. Johns Road
Isleworth
Middlesex TW7 6NJ
Tel: (020) 8568 5733
www.lavendersoflondon.co.uk
Artificial plants, silk and dried flowers,
florist's sundries

Norbury Farm Flower Centre
Jackson's Lane
Hazel Grove
Stockport
Cheshire SK7 5JS
Tel: (0161) 483 8284
www.norburyfarm.com
Silk, dried, latex and parchment
flowers and foliage, ceramics,
baskets, fruits, sundries

Pene Dene Flowers
Sigwells
Sherbourne
Dorset DT9 4LN
Tel: (01963) 220 460
www.penedene.com
Silk flowers and foliage

Smithers Oasis (UK) Ltd
Crowther Road
Crowther Industrial Estate
Washington
Tyne & Wear
NE38 0AQ
Tel: (0191) 417 5595
Manufacturers of accessories
for flower arranging, including
wreath frames and oasis foam

AUSTRALIA

Acacia Art Florist
24 Commercial Road
Port Augusta
SA 5700
Tel: (08) 8642 2559

Cherub's Craft and Art Supplies
243 Main Road
Blackwood
SA 5051
Tel: (08) 8278 1244

Danish Flower Art
Mail Service 582
New England Highway
Highfields
QLD 4352
Tel: (07) 4630 8211

Lincraft
Head Office
31–33 Alfred Street
Blackburn
VIC 3130
Tel: (03) 9875 7575

Mosmania
776 Military Road
Mosman
NSW 2088
Tel: (02) 9969 7467

Norwest Craft Supplies
Unit 3/5 Warambie Road
Karratha
WA 6714
Tel: (08) 9144 4059

Spotlight
Head Office
100 Market Street
South Melbourne
VIC 3205
Tel: (03) 9690 8899

Stonleigh Flowers
49 High Street
Wodonga
VIC 3689
Tel: (02) 6024 7307
Email: stonleigh@hotkey.net.au
Fresh, dried, silk and artificial
flowers

Sweet Violets Mosman
773 Military Road
Mosman
NSW 2088
Tel/Fax: (02) 9969 9381
Fresh and silk flowers, urns and vases

Temples Floral Sundries
55 Vore Street
Silverwater
NSW 2128
Tel: (02) 9748 2666

NEW ZEALAND

Flower Systems Ltd
391 Neilson Street
Penrose
Auckland
Tel: (09) 622 1728
Fax: (09) 622 8996
Email: delboy@clear.net.nz

Alison's Acquisitions
390 Parnell Road
Parnell
Auckland
Tel: (09) 373 2904

Auckland Flower Wholesalers
761 Great South Road
Penrose
Tel: (09) 579 5692
Wide selection of floristry equipment

Floral Expressions
38 Buxton Square
Nelson
Tel: (03) 546 8978
Freephone: 0508 783 539
Fax: (03) 546 8978

Tree Makers
231 Annex Road
Riccarton
Christchurch
Tel/Fax: (03) 338 9484
www.treemakers.co.nz

Spotlight Stores
Stores in the following locations:
Christchurch
Hamilton
Hastings
Manukau City
New Plymouth
Palmerston North
Panmure
Porirua
Rotorua
South Dunedin
Wairau Park
Wellington
Freephone: 0800 276 222 for more details
www.spotlightonline.co.nz

index

INDEX COMPILED BY MARIE LORIMER

author's acknowledgements

I would like to thank Susan Berry for her support and encouragement, and for putting together a talented and professional team, who were also a pleasure to work with. I would like to thank John Heseltine and Anne Wilson, respectively, for the excellent photography and design. I am also grateful to New Holland, in particular Rosemary Wilkinson and Clare Hubbard, for their editorial input.

www.alientechnology.com

ALL-9354-02

www.alientechnology.com

ALL-9354-02

www.alientechnology.com

ALL-9354-02